T0129909

I CHOOSE ME

ONE WOMAN'S JOURNEY BACK TO SELF

BRENDA M WOOD

BALBOA.PRESS
A DIVISION OF HAY HOUSE

Copyright © 2020 Brenda M Wood.

All rights reserved. No part of this book may be used or reproduced by
any means, graphic, electronic or mechanical, including photocopying,
recording, taping or by any information storage retrieval system
without the written permission of the author except in the case
of brief quotations embodied in critical articles and reviews.

This book is a work of non-fiction. Unless otherwise noted, the author
and the publisher make no explicit guarantees as to the accuracy of
the information contained in this book and in some cases, names of
people and places have been altered to protect their privacy.

Balboa Press books may be ordered through booksellers or by contacting:

Balboa Press
A Division of Hay House
1663 Liberty Drive
Bloomington, IN 47403
www.balboapress.com
1 (877) 407-4847

Because of the dynamic nature of the Internet, any web addresses or
links contained in this book may have changed since publication and
may no longer be valid. The views expressed in this work are solely those
of the author and do not necessarily reflect the views of the publisher,
and the publisher hereby disclaims any responsibility for them.

The author of this book does not dispense medical advice or prescribe the use
of any technique as a form of treatment for physical, emotional or medical
problems without the advice of a physician, either directly or indirectly. The
intent of the author is only to offer information of a general nature to help
you in your quest for emotional and spiritual well-being. In the event you use
any of the information in this book for yourself, which is your constitutional
right, the author and the publisher assume no responsibility for your actions.

Any people depicted in stock imagery provided by Getty Images are
models, and such images are being used for illustrative purposes only.
Certain stock imagery © Getty Images.

Print information available on the last page.

ISBN: 978-1-9822-4919-9 (sc)
ISBN: 978-1-9822-4920-5 (e)

Balboa Press rev. date: 07/08/2020

For my inner child

Thank you for hanging in there.

I love you.

A special thanks to Jennifer Kubiak, my line editor with KN Literary Arts, for her amazing editing skills, her well-placed suggestions and her encouragement to stretch beyond what I thought I was capable of.

Preface

Dear reader,

When the idea to write this book first came to me, I wondered why anyone would be interested in reading what I had to say. I knew that I had been through some extremely difficult experiences, some of which included my 29-year-old son getting killed in a car accident, the inevitable passing of loved ones, going through a bankruptcy, surviving thyroid cancer by having my thyroid removed and experiencing that one single life-changing event that was the catalyst for my life being propelled in a completely different direction: I discovered that my husband of 22 years was a sexual predator. What if, by sharing my story, I could help someone else?

As I was taking notes and trying to decide how I wanted to say everything that I wanted to say, I started noticing a pattern in the thoughts that kept coming to mind. I kept remembering all the positive things that got me through the difficult times, the instances of hope and guidance that revealed themselves to me, like bright nuggets of truth to follow, leading me out of the darkness. My biggest surprise was what started as a journey of survival turned into an inner journey that led me to me, a journey that I will forever be grateful for.

We all have our own stories in which the details are different, and the same. Not everyone handles things in the same way—that's personal choice. My prayer for you, dear reader, is that you find a way to allow the light within you (it is there!) to guide you out of any darkness you may be going through. You are not alone! Dare to believe in yourself, and start your own journey of self-discovery, a hero's journey. Everything you need is already within you, no matter what outer appearances may look like. Take back your power and find your voice. A journey of this much importance is never easy, but it is so worth it. Keep pushing through, and you will be amazed at the discoveries that await you.

If anything in the story you are about to read helps you in any way, I will have accomplished what I set out to do. It truly is never too late to find your way! I am 64 years young, and I feel such hope for my future. I am ready!

Brenda M Wood
April 2020

1

This Is My Life?

Have you ever looked around at your life and wondered how you got there? Do you feel stuck, like you are perpetually reliving the same day, the same year, over and over, with nothing ever changing or getting better? If so, read on. You will see that it is possible for you to make positive changes.

My Path: In the Beginning

I grew up in a middle-class family, the oldest of four children. I was a very shy, sensitive child, always prone to crying at the drop of a hat. As a family unit, we were all extremely close, but as a couple, Mom and Dad had a troubled marriage. They worked hard to shield us kids from their problems, but we could hear them arguing after we went to bed. They were just human, trying to do the best they could.

They were great parents. They loved us kids so much, making sure that we were a close-knit family filled with love. There was a lot of laughter in our house, with quality family time together. Mom and Dad instilled in each one of us a sense of humor. My parents gave me the foundation of knowing that there is always a better way of looking at things, and I am grateful for that. I did not always remember this, but it was there in the background, ready to surface when I truly needed it. Sometimes laughter can make all the difference. Laughter may not change your circumstances, but it can change how you feel by releasing stress or creating an opening for hope to grow.

My siblings and I were not perfect by any means. We had all the usual squabbles and rivalries that kids have. Even though I never talked about it, I often felt like an ugly duckling when I was growing up. My younger sister was so beautiful, and although she herself never did or said anything for me to feel this way, I remember feeling insecure and lacking around her, like I was never quite good enough. I'm sure that, on some level, this is probably a common rivalry between sisters growing up. Who knows how or why these feelings found a resting place within me, creating false notions and beliefs about myself that would play out, unchallenged, in my life for many years. But from that point on, I always felt that I had to do something to earn the love of others, like I had to be perfect so no one would know that I didn't quite measure up. I was always trying to prove myself and always feeling like I had to do everything myself. It was like a silent computer program constantly running in the background, affecting every thought, every decision, every action. It's an exhausting way to live!

By the time I was 17, my insecurities were fully intact. And they grew worse when, as I was getting ready to enter my senior year of high school, Dad moved our family out of state. I was devastated. We moved again less than a year later, so I ended up going to two different high schools in my senior year.

Too Young

Soon after my family and I moved and had gotten settled into our first of two homes, the company that my dad worked for decided to do some advertising. It hired teenagers to be part of a crew that passed brochures door-to-door. My parents gave permission for me to be part of this so I could earn some extra spending money. It was summertime, and the company had no trouble finding enough kids to participate.

It was there where I met the young man who was to become my first husband. I was 17, and he was 18. We started dating soon after we met and then into my senior year. The fact that I had a boyfriend helped buffer the sadness of missing all my friends back home.

Halfway through my senior year, my parents moved our family to a different house located on the other side of town. Unfortunately, it was in a different school district, which meant starting over again at a new school just a few months before graduation.

The changes unsettled me. There was still love in our family, but Mom and Dad both had full-time jobs, and my siblings were also teenagers with their own lives. I found myself clinging to my relationship with my boyfriend. We started talking about getting married and ended up eloping in the spring, right before an uneventful graduation.

At the time, marriage seemed like the answer to my prayers, a steady rock in a turbulent sea. In hindsight, I was so naïve and inexperienced, too young to be getting married. The marriage turned out to be emotionally abusive. It felt like my husband had changed into a completely different person as soon as we were married. There was infidelity on his part almost from the beginning. There was also constant arguing, and all I ever heard was how worthless I was.

I wanted so desperately for this marriage to work, and I felt like it was time to do what married couples do: Have a baby. After much convincing, my husband agreed. Our daughter was born two years into the marriage.

Nothing changed much between my husband and me after the baby came, but I discovered that I loved being a mother, and I was so grateful to have my beautiful daughter. I loved motherhood so much that I wanted to have a second child. Again, it took a lot of convincing, but my husband finally agreed. Our son was born two years after his sister.

Six months into my pregnancy with our son, my husband decided that he preferred his many infidelities over our life together and had me served with divorce papers. There had been no prior discussion, and he was still living at home, so I was totally blindsided.

His attorney, having not been informed that I was pregnant, refused to represent my husband when that fact became known. My husband and I did, however, separate. I asked my mom, who was divorced from my dad by this time, if I could move in with her, but she said no.

When my husband found out what she had said, his response was, "See, no one wants you!" Isn't it amazing how life mirrors back what is going on within us?

I later found out that my mother was trying to force my husband into taking some sort of responsibility, but I had never felt so alone in my entire life. Eventually, my mom apologized to me, and I did stay with her for a while. Over the next two years, my husband and I got back together and split up a few more times.

When I reflect on what moved me to make the final break, I cannot recall a specific incident. I believe that, out of sheer emotional exhaustion, I had just had enough! In order to let go, I had to get to the point where I felt that anything would be better than this. It was time. My theme song became "I Will Survive," sung by Gloria Gaynor.

Husband No. 2

During one of my separations from my first husband, I met a nice man named Bob, who worked at the same place that I did. We had great conversations, and I eventually agreed to go to a movie with him one evening. Unfortunately, soon after, I ended up reuniting with my husband again. My husband didn't want me, but he didn't want anyone else to have me either, so I lost touch with this nice man. It would be three years before I spoke to Bob again.

When I was finally divorced, Bob crossed my mind. I contacted him, we started dating and we ended up marrying. We had our daughter three years later. It was during this period of my life that I started my emotional healing. My new husband knew how deeply wounded I was. He was loving, patient and just what I needed.

Two important things came out of this time of my life: discovering spirituality, and singing. I had always loved God and church. My dad never pushed me, my sister or my two brothers into going to church when we were kids because our mom never wanted to go. But every Sunday morning, he got up, announced that he was going to church and asked if anyone wanted to go with him. I don't think I ever missed a Sunday at church with my dad. It felt like our special time together, and I will forever cherish those moments.

Fast-forward to my second marriage. Dad had been reading a book about reincarnation and let me borrow it when he was finished. The ideas in this book really sparked an interest in me about life and other ways to look at it. Then a friend of mine introduced me to the book *Illusions* by Richard Bach. This book changed my life, and it created more questions in my mind. How could I wrap my mind around the idea that we are all spiritual beings having a human experience, and what did that mean in my life? How could I feel worthy enough to think that the spark of God lives and breathes in me and that it is God's great pleasure for me to be, do and have anything I want? How could I let go of my victim mentality and take responsibility for everything in my life?

Thus, my spiritual journey had begun. I became ravenous for information. I read metaphysical books that spoke to me. Some of the books included *The Dragon Doesn't Live Here Anymore* by Alan Cohen, *The Superbeings* by John Randolph Price, *You Can Heal Your*

Life by Louise Hay, *The Power of Intention* by Wayne Dyer and *The Law of Attraction* by Esther and Jerry Hicks. There was a minister on the radio every morning when I drove to work whose short spot was called "Word of the Day." I found that when I focused on that one word and let it guide my day, my day always went better. His church, Unity Church, was just a few blocks from my husband's workplace. My friend and I decided to try it out one Sunday. I was home!! The church was based on spirituality and the teachings of Jesus, and it embraced the ideas found within the books that I had been reading. Although my childhood church had served me well for a time, the study of spirituality was to be the next step of my journey.

It was at Unity Church where, although I was nervous to take the initiative, I took a brave step forward and joined the choir. I had loved singing my entire life but had gotten away from it during the tumultuous beginning of my adulthood. It felt so good to be singing again! I vowed to myself that I would continue to sing no matter what, honoring that gift in me that touched my heart and soul. To this day, although not at the same Unity Church that I started in, I am still attending a Unity Church. My current church, which I have been attending for over 20 years now, has a band that provides the weekly music and I am so blessed and grateful to be singing with them.

My husband, Bob, who was open-minded and of his own accord, started reading some of the spiritual books that I had read. I think he was a little surprised at how interesting he found them and that he agreed with the concepts discussed. We spent many an hour having deep, thought-provoking conversations. It was a happy time.

Alas, change is inevitable. We had been married for nine years when my husband had a heart attack, suffered complications from major bypass surgery and hovered, in a state the doctor described as being brain-dead, for two weeks before dying. I was 35 years old, and our daughter, who had just been diagnosed with autism, was 6.

Although my spiritual beliefs helped and I was able to draw some comfort from the thought that we are all spiritual beings having a human experience and there is no death, just a transition back to Spirit, I was also struggling with my human emotions at the death of my husband. I was knee-deep in reality. I spoke to one of my Unity ministers following my husband's transition, telling her that I was trying so hard to hold onto truths during this time. She told me to stop and just let myself feel what I was going through, that I needed to let myself grieve. I was relieved. It was okay to feel however I was feeling.

His passing happened a few weeks before Christmas, and all I wanted to do was pull the covers over my head and cry. I never hurt so much in my life! I barely got the kids and myself through Christmas that year. I was grateful to my minister for the advice that she had given me. My grief was so intense I could not imagine what holding it inside would have done. There was something so healing about letting the tears flow.

A person can remain in this state for only so long. About three weeks after my husband's death, I began sensing internally that it was no longer serving me to stay immersed in my sorrow. I had had enough of being in such pain! My time of extreme grieving was not that long, according to the calendar. I know the length of this process is different for each person, but for me, living it moment by moment, day in and day out, had been debilitating. I had cried all my tears, and now I was just reliving the pain. I had children to raise, and they were depending on me. I remember saying to myself, "I do not like how this feels, and I no longer want to be in this pain." Somehow, that thought flipped a switch inside me, and even though I was still sad and missed my husband terribly, the days started to get a little brighter, and I was able to focus on other things instead of letting my grief take over my every waking hour. I started to feel like me again.

Husband No. 3

The same week after Christmas that I had allowed myself to come out from under this dark cloud, a friend of Bob's, whom I had known for years, invited me out to dinner, saying that I needed to get out of the house for a while. I accepted his invitation. Because we had known each other for so long, it was easy to fall into a relationship. We ended up marrying about six months later.

I had such hope for this, my third marriage. My first husband had been so cruel, and, although sweet and kind, my second husband had been quite passive. This new husband felt like someone whom I could walk beside, not behind or in front of.

In the beginning, we laughed a lot. He always felt like he had to be the life of the party, which was probably one of the things that attracted me to him. But as time went by, I noticed that although he was still the life of the party and made everybody think that he was this great guy who couldn't get enough of his wife, it was all a front.

He was a restaurant manager and would leave for work before I got home in the evening, and then I was asleep when he got home in the middle of the night. Our moments of intimacy were few and far between. At first, I thought it was just our schedules, and I enjoyed the weekends when we were both home at the same time.

But over time, he became less and less attentive. I kept asking what was wrong; was it me? He always said it was him, not me, with no explanation. But it never got better. Eventually, I discovered that he had diabetes and that impotence was one of the side effects. I told him that I understood, but he would get angry and insist that he didn't have that problem.

I wanted us to work together, to be a couple and to be able to handle, together, anything that came our way. I would have settled for affection, an occasional hug, a kiss, sitting close while watching television, meaningful conversation, any action that would signify that love was still present, that we still mattered to each other. But there was only distance. I felt like we were just roommates, not a married couple.

Right in the middle of this time of our marriage, my two oldest granddaughters came to live with us. They were ages 6 and 4 at the time. Having something else to focus on, I gladly embraced this new responsibility and poured my love and care into these two little ones who needed me. We all settled into a routine. There was work, school and kids growing up and all that that entails. Unfortunately, there was no change between my husband and me. Although we appeared to be a normal couple, underneath it all, there was no real closeness.

I Can't Take Much More!

Fifteen years into my third marriage, my 28-year-old son disappeared. He had been unhappy for quite a while, struggling with different issues. It took me a couple weeks of not knowing where he was before I started to suspect that something was wrong, as opposed to him choosing to go off by himself. What tipped me off was the fact that other family members and friends had started asking if we had seen or heard from him. Following my oldest daughter's suggestion, I contacted the police where he lived so they could go check his house for clues. I also let them know that he had a dog. I would have gone myself, but I was afraid of what I might find there.

The police called me back and said that no one was inside, including the dog. The mail was stacked up quite a bit. It had been several days since he had been there. There was no sign of foul play, and since my son was an adult, there was nothing else they could do.

Now what? Although concerned, I was relieved at what they found. It could have been so much worse! With the new information that the police had provided, I felt like my son was okay, but for some reason, he had felt the need to leave with no word. Since he wasn't answering his phone, I had no choice but to wait for him to contact me.

A few days later, while I was at work, my phone rang. It was my son!! "Is my picture on a milk carton yet?" he asked.

"Almost!" I said.

He was in California. He said that he had dreams and that he didn't want anyone to tell him he couldn't pursue them, so he just left. I suspected there was much more to the story, but I was so relieved he was okay that nothing else mattered!

Over the next few months, we talked often on the phone. He told me about friends he had made, things he was doing and how beautiful it was there. He even mentioned that I should come out there to visit him. It was good to hear him sounding settled and moving on with his life. My worries about him eased up a bit.

At home in my world, it was busy, as usual. On top of working a full-time job and raising my youngest daughter, along with my two granddaughters, I was active in my church, going to band rehearsal every Thursday evening and singing during the service every Sunday morning. Praying that God would watch over my son to keep him safe, I was always careful to shield the girls from any concerns I had.

Then came my son's 29th birthday. I tried repeatedly to get in touch with him that day but failed. With each attempt, I became more and more afraid that some physical harm had befallen him. I felt utterly helpless because he was so far away. Finally, a few days later, he called me. He seemed to be in good spirits. After being so worried about him, I said, "Not to be morbid, but if something would happen to you, does anybody out there have my number and would know to call me?" He promised he would give my number to his roommate. That made me feel better, and that was also the last time I spoke to my son.

Two weeks later, there was a message on my phone from his roommate, asking me to call. When I called back, he informed me that my son had been killed in a car accident the night before. Up to that point in my life, I had only had to deal with the death of a spouse, which was devastating. The death of my son was pain beyond words.

The next few days were a blur with so many calls to family and friends, so many retellings of the details and arrangements made to have him cremated and sent home.

In addition to the call from my son's roommate, I received a call from the deputy who was at the scene. He was extremely caring when relaying to me the details as he knew them, and he answered all my questions to the best of his ability. As his mother, one of the hardest parts of dealing with the loss of my son was not knowing how he spent his last hours and minutes. There were still gaps in how my son spent his last day on this Earth, and I was determined to get answers so I could find some sort of closure.

I spoke to the girl who he was seeing out there. She was able to tell me how they spent the day and what events had led up to him driving on that mountain road that night. I found out from the deputy that his car had gone over a cliff, which was six feet high, but he was found on the side of the road. Someone had heard his cries for help and called 911. He was still alive when the paramedics arrived, but they couldn't save him. I know that it doesn't change the outcome, but it's a comfort to know he was not alone when he died.

I even spoke to a kind woman at the morgue where he was being kept. Again, I knew it didn't change anything, but because I was hoping he hadn't suffered, I wanted to know what condition his body was in. She assured me that he showed no external injuries. They were all internal.

I was so grateful to everyone who filled in their part of the details. But I discovered, during all of this, something much worse than having to listen to strangers speak of things no mother wants to hear. That something is the *unknown*, the place where fear and one's imagination resides. There are no boundaries, nothing to rein in one's thoughts. It can drive a person crazy because no matter what scenario one comes up with, it's still the unknown. At least if one has facts, they can be processed, and closure can eventually be attained.

One thing that was still bothering me was the fact that I did not know what happened at the moment of the accident. How could I possibly ever know those details? That did not stop me from praying for answers. I just kept asking to be shown what happened, and I got a miracle.

One night, I had a dream. In my dream, I saw my son jump out of his car as it was going over the cliff. Because it was dark, he had no idea how far down the cliff went, and he had jumped out of his car to save his own life. His internal injuries occurred when his unprotected body hit the ground. I woke up and just kept running the dream through my mind. I knew it was just a dream, but it was closure that I could live with. I learned that when I sincerely ask for answers, believe and keep an open mind, Spirit shows me the answers in a way that is easiest for me to understand. I just have to pay attention. Thank you, God, for answered prayers!

But that's not the end of the story. One day, I received the police report in the mail. It looked very official. I proceeded to read it, and then I stopped. I reread the part that described the car that my son was driving and what clothes he was wearing at the time of the accident. Both descriptions were exactly what I saw in my dream, to the last detail! I had no idea what car he had driven to California! And I could not have known what clothes he would have chosen to wear on any given day! Again, thank you, God, for reinforcing the answer that I prayed for and for helping me to be open enough to receive it!! That's proof enough for me!

Circle of Life

That was a sad year for our family. Three months after my son died, my maternal grandmother got sick and died at the age of 87. The loss of a loved one is never easy, but we were all gifted with time. Except for near the end, Grandma was conscious and able to carry on conversations. Every single family member was able to have private time with her and say everything they needed to say. We all had a chance to say goodbye. Then, when her time came, she quietly slipped away.

In a quiet moment after my grandmother's death, I found myself reflecting over the last three months and the two deaths in the family, both of which were completely different experiences. One was a tragic injustice, devastating and hard to accept. The other was a part of life, natural and surrounded with love. They were both equally loved, and they both left their bodies and merged back into Spirit. What made the difference? I felt that if I could answer that question, I would gain another tool that would help me navigate life. And then it came to me in one word: *closure!* I thought about how hard I had searched for closure when my son died. It was at the point when I received this precious gift that I could accept and move on. With my grandmother, closure was attained before she died. That's what made her passing so peaceful in the minds of her loved ones. What a wonderful gift this knowledge is, a welcome light shining on the path while traveling through the darkest grief. Thank you, God!

Heading in the Right Direction

The next six years were spent in financial terror. As time passed, my husband and I slipped into deep debt. We were unable to pay our bills on time, and we never answered the phone because of bill collectors. The whole situation seemed hopeless, with no end in sight!

Then a ray of sunshine made its way into our world. As much as we hated the thought of having to do it, we felt like we had no other recourse. We filed for bankruptcy.

The process was less than enjoyable—it included finding an attorney, answering all the questions, filling out all the paperwork, figuring out exactly everything that we owed and having to take and pass online courses. We forged ahead and, finally, the day came when our debt was discharged. That was the first time in years that we could breathe easily. The load was gone from our shoulders! Now it was time to rebuild.

My Dad, My Rock

About four months after the bankruptcy was final, my dad was diagnosed with cancer. Less than two months later, he was gone. He was 80 when he died.

As soon as we found out that Dad was sick, our whole family made every effort to spend as much time with him as we could. He was already sharing a house with my sister and brother. I will forever be grateful to them for all the love and caring they gave him! They, selflessly and around the clock, saw to his every need and honored his wishes to stay at home.

Where do I even begin to speak of the love and respect that I had and have for this man? He was my dad! From my earliest memories, he was always so strong, so loving, so quick to laugh. I can remember when my siblings and I were little, Dad would play "monster" with us. He would lie on the couch pretending to be asleep. Very quietly, we would creep up on him, and just when we were about to pounce, he would grab us, make monster noises and tickle us unmercifully. He was also known to "beard" us by scraping his unshaved chin across our little cheeks, making us squeal. There were so many wonderful moments of love and laughter.

Dad was also the wisest man I knew. I learned, from an early age, that I could count on him to give an honest, well-thought-out response to whatever advice

I was seeking. He never gave a knee-jerk answer, and no question was too silly or too small. He was my hero throughout my life, including when I, as a little child, asked him what made the skin on cuticles tear, or when I cried to him when I was in grade school because my friends were ignoring me and I asked him what I should do. He was the first parent I told when I started my period, and on my 18th birthday, he came home from work with a bouquet of flowers for me, my first. I remember telling him one time that, as a dad, he reminded me of the character that Andy Griffith portrayed on *The Andy Griffith Show* a father who was so thoughtful and caring. He thanked me, not quite sure what to say, but the love that shone in his eyes was priceless!

After Dad received his diagnosis, he was open about discussing with my siblings and me all his thoughts and fears about facing the upcoming end of his physical life. We also shared with him about how we were feeling. As hard as it was to talk about such things, Dad remained true to himself to the very end—open, honest and loving.

I will always remember the night before Dad passed. Days earlier, hospice had set him up in a hospital bed in his living room. Now, for the last few days, there was no communication from him. He lay there quietly, with the appearance of being unconscious. That evening, our whole family was seated around Dad, and it didn't take long for us to start doing what we do best—laugh and tell stories. We couldn't help ourselves! We just kept reminiscing and laughing, laughing and reminiscing.

And then it happened. My youngest brother looked over at Dad, who was grinning from ear to ear! It was a most precious moment. Dad had heard everything we were saying! He may have appeared to be unconscious, but he was present, in the midst of us, enjoying his family like he always did.

We are all grateful that we had that last wonderful evening with Dad. He died the next day, waiting until we were all out of the room before he left.

Life: What Next?

Up to this point, I had indeed been through many difficult experiences, but so have you. Each one of us on this path called life has been molded and influenced by our experiences. Although the timing and details may be different, we all have moments of normalcy, love, tragedy, comic relief, boredom, triumph and despair. And there are lessons in every bit of it. The wonderful thing is, if we let one lesson get away, we can always count on the universe to send it back around as many times as it takes until we allow ourselves to learn that specific lesson.

Sometimes when we are in the middle of living an experience, it's not always easy to see the big picture, so we just do the best we can in every moment. I was still feeling like I was doomed to continue down the same path with my marriage. What could possibly happen that would make a difference? I was about to find out.

2

Time to Wake Up

Have you ever been going along in your day, a day like any other day, and suddenly been blindsided with news so horrific that you felt that it couldn't possibly be true, news that changed your life forever?

Cosmic Two-by-Four!

"Hello, this is your granddaughter's principal. She's having a really bad day today. It was reported that she was molested in your home and the grandfather did it. She is talking to the police right now."

When I received that phone call, life would never again be the same. It was the beginning of a chain of events that would propel my life and the lives of my granddaughters in a totally different direction.

I will not speak of specific details out of respect for my granddaughters, but after several meetings with the police detectives, Child Protective Services and psychologists, it was determined that my husband had been inappropriately touching my granddaughters for years. The police were able to obtain a confession from him, he had his day in court and he was sentenced to prison as a sexual predator, where he has since passed away.

First Things First

I was going to write that my granddaughters are now strong young women, which they truly are, but they have always been strong. They had to be in order to endure the endless nightmare that they were caught in. They each have had their struggles to overcome the emotional and psychological damage that my third husband caused, and they have made progress in their healing, each on their own path.

I love them, support them and am so proud of them for their strength and courage. That being said, their journey is just that—their journey. I can only speak of my own experience throughout this ordeal, but I did talk to them prior to writing this chapter and was given their full permission to say what I needed to say.

Healing: Where to Begin?

Have you ever had a tangled skein of yarn or fishing line where you can't find the beginning or the end and have no idea where to start to untangle the mess? That's exactly how I was feeling in the aftermath of the terrible news about my husband. My emotions were all over the place; I had a million different questions but no answers.

The first thing I did was to get in his face, screaming, "Why? Why? Answer me!!! *Why?*"

Of course, he had no answer. Not only did he do unthinkable things to my granddaughters, which is beyond vile, but he betrayed me, his wife. His sexual preferences, unknown to me, had affected our relationship for years. His constant indifference influenced my self-esteem. "Has our entire marriage been a lie?!" I asked.

"Yeah, pretty much," were his exact words to me.

That was 22 years of my life that I would never get back. I might have been able to better deal with the jumble of emotions that were running rampant inside me if he would have apologized or shown any remorse, but he did neither. One of my granddaughters confided in me that, before he was arrested, he went so far as to accuse her of ruining his life. White-hot anger shot through me! The girls and I were all dealing with so much hurt. How would we ever get past this?

I also found that I had a hard time looking at pictures of my granddaughters when they were little. My poor babies! How could he? All I could think about was: What was he doing with them at this age? Or this age? Or this age?

This also triggered some feelings of guilt in me for not being able to protect them from him. I was talking to one of my granddaughters one day about how I was feeling, and she said to me, "Nanny, you were never present when he did anything." I know she's right, and I recognize that the girls don't blame me. I just know that I am so grateful for the close relationship that my granddaughters and I have. We have grown even closer throughout all of this. Thank you, God!

Before he was sentenced, I obtained a divorce and had my last name changed back to my previous married name. I did *not* want to be associated with his last name in any way, shape or form.

My granddaughters and I were asked to write a victim impact statement, and when the court date arrived, we were asked to read them to the judge, telling how our lives were impacted by what he had done. I was asked to go first. As I spoke the words that I needed to say, I watched my ex-husband's face. He never looked at me, and he seemed like he was trying to keep from crying. When I was finished, he was given the opportunity to say something. He chose silence.

Due to extenuating circumstances, my oldest granddaughter was unable to be present, but her younger sister bravely stood up and read her statement. I was heartbroken to hear her words. She spoke of things that I was unaware of, things that were hard to listen to. As I looked around the room, noticing the tears in many eyes as my granddaughter spoke, my ex still had the same look on his face, not looking up, and choosing silence when given the chance to speak.

There was one more statement given that day. My granddaughters' other grandmother wanted to speak. She had nothing written down, but she spoke from her heart. She talked of betrayed trust and other things, mirroring everything that the rest of us were feeling. I was grateful for her honesty and bravery.

It was the judge's turn to speak next. He spoke at length and then handed down a sentence. The last time I saw my ex-husband, he was being led down the hall in shackles. At that moment, I felt nothing, having endured emotional extremes for months. I was numb. I just watched as he walked out of my life.

One Day at a Time

From the moment I found out what my husband had done, I felt trapped in a swirl of thoughts and emotions. At any given point of the day I would just keep replaying everything in my head over and over. I would be driving to work, and I would get so angry that I would just start screaming. If I wasn't screaming, sometimes I would just cry. I felt out of control and powerless to stop the direction of my thoughts.

Then one evening a short time after my husband was sentenced, my sanity returned. From all my spiritual studies, I knew about the power of thoughts and the law of attraction. I knew that thoughts reproduce similar thoughts, and I knew that whatever you place your attention on expands. I had been completely focusing on the hurt instead of on the healing. This aha moment was a turning point for me.

Once I reached that turning point, I focused on what healing would look like for me. The word *forgiveness* was the first thing that came to mind, but I didn't know where to begin. I had heard that forgiveness is the act of consciously choosing to let go of hurt caused by someone, but not condoning or excusing what they did. It is an act of self-love that releases us from the situation so we may heal.

One day when I was thinking about how to work on the forgiveness that was so desperately needed, a thought came to mind. I had heard the following saying many times: "What you think of me is none of my business." So, if what you think of me is none of my business, that means that what I think of you is none of your business. I need to say that again! What I think of you is none of your business. Wow! After calling my now ex-husband every name in the book, that realization placed my feelings right back into my own lap; they were my responsibility. But I found this very empowering. My feelings were totally within my own control, no one else's. It took me out of victim mode.

Another process that helped me tremendously was contemplating the law of attraction and applying it to my own situation, which was so emotionally charged that forgiveness would have been unattainable from that state of victimhood.

I knew instinctively that in order to diffuse the situation in my thoughts, I would have to look at it from a neutral place, to somehow take the personalities out of the equation.

The law of attraction, as stated in *The Law of Attraction* by Esther and Jerry Hicks, is exemplified by: "That which is like unto itself, is drawn." The entire universe is made up of energy, and we are all vibrational beings. Our thoughts and emotions all vibrate at different levels, positive emotions being higher vibrations and negative emotions being lower vibrations.

The law of attraction is constantly matching things up that are of like vibration. It is totally impartial.

I had no idea what my granddaughters and I each had going on in our own vibrations that had brought us into that situation, and I didn't need to figure that part out. It was enough just to know what was going on from that different perspective. I still didn't condone anything that my ex-husband did, but when I approached my forgiveness process from this perspective, I was able to release myself emotionally in order to start healing. He had already been held accountable for his actions, and that was none of my business.

My job now was to work on myself. I knew for sure that if I didn't want to keep attracting the same type of experiences into my life, I would need to change my own vibration.

Things Are Looking Up

I chose to immerse myself in spiritual self-help books to help improve my frame of mind. I also took a class at church. The class helped tremendously because not only was I spending time with like-minded people, but there were great discussions every week, one of which was about forgiveness.

I had finally turned a corner, and although I would never forget what had transpired, I was able to put this part of my life behind me and start living in the present.

3

Speak Up! I Can't Hear You!

Have you ever felt like you didn't have a voice, or that it would be easier to just keep quiet? To not confront, to not make waves, to keep the peace? We can spend a lifetime feeling this way, but at what cost?

Blessings in Disguise

The next life lesson to show up on my journey was the discovery that thoughts and feelings that I hold onto, especially the ones I am emotional about and hold as true, can show up as physical symptoms in my body. Thoughts held in mind produce after their kind. Where could a symptom possibly show up in my body if I had trouble expressing myself and saying how I really felt? Since the throat chakra is the center of communication and creativity, you guessed it: my thyroid!

Spirit uses absolutely everything in our lives to bring good to us. We may not always see it or recognize it for the blessing that it is. We may even curse events that occur, calling them bad luck and wondering, "Why me?" Believe me, I have had my share of those responses.

I had been having nosebleeds for several months— not all the time, but somewhat regularly. They were inconvenient, but there was no pain involved. I finally decided that they were not going to go away, so I made an appointment to see my family doctor. The examination did not provide any answers, and my doctor was unable to see any cause for the nosebleeds. It was suggested that I see an ear, nose and throat specialist. The ENT doctor was thorough in his examination and discovered that there was a tiny little bump inside my nose that, over time, had been cracking and bleeding. He said that he could cauterize it, which should take care of the problem. He performed the procedure then and there, and I thought we were done. I guess because of the nature of his specialty, he then started feeling around on my throat. He told me that he felt a definite lump in my thyroid. I was told that I should see an endocrinologist to have it checked out.

The endocrinologist started off by doing some bloodwork and then feeling around on my neck in the area of my thyroid. He confirmed that I had a nodule that was large enough to be detected just by physical touch. But once he reviewed the results of my ultrasound, he didn't feel that there was anything to worry about.

When my bloodwork came back, the doctor informed me that I had an underactive thyroid (hypothyroidism) and an autoimmune disease called Hashimoto's thyroiditis. The way Hashimoto's was described to me was that the immune system views the thyroid as a foreign object and starts attacking it.

The next step was to do a biopsy of the nodule. Even though the doctor wasn't too concerned about it being malignant, the biopsy would tell us for sure what we were dealing with. This procedure was uncomfortable at best. I was told not to swallow as a very long needle was inserted through my neck into the nodule, and tissue was extracted to be sent off for testing. When the results came back, I was told that not enough tissue had been retrieved to determine whether or not the nodule was benign. A second biopsy was recommended and performed, and again, we got the same results—not enough tissue to be conclusive. I was not pleased!

Two choices were suggested to me. One choice was to wait six months, to have another biopsy done and go from there. The second choice was surgery to have my thyroid removed. First, I wanted to be proactive and stay on top of the situation, not just sit around and wait. Also, I had already been through two uncomfortable biopsy procedures, to no avail. Last, I felt that my thyroid was already damaged due to the Hashimoto's and that it wasn't going to get any better. I had been having extreme exhaustion for a long time, on top of other symptoms. Thus, I made the decision to have my thyroid removed.

I was given the names of a couple of surgeons to choose from, one of whom was my ENT doctor. Since I already knew him and also found out that he was one of the best surgeons around, I enlisted him to perform the surgery. Everything was set to go.

When the day came for my surgery, I was nervous. Earlier, I had repeatedly stressed to my surgeon that I was a singer and to please be extra careful! Singing in my church band was a source of pure joy for me. It had also been a lifeline, seeing me through many difficult times in my life. Now, when faced with this upcoming surgery, the surgery's possible effect on my vocal cords was on my mind more than the removal of my thyroid. That's how much I loved singing!

Other than having my tonsils removed when I was in grade school and going through childbirth three times, I had not been in the hospital for any other procedures. I was very nervous.

The anesthesiologist came in to speak to me and take me down to surgery. I remember thinking that he seemed young. Needing to lighten my mood, I felt like the situation called for a healthy dose of humor. So, as I lay on the gurney while being wheeled down the hallway, I asked him if he had ever had surgery (I wanted to know if he could relate to what I was experiencing). He told me that he had been fortunate to have never been in that position. "I wouldn't be so worried about my surgery if it was concerning a limb or something," I said as I held up both my hands, flipping them at the wrist for emphasis while moving my head with attitude. "But when someone is coming at your throat with a knife, it makes one a little nervous." As soon as the words were out of my mouth, he let out a surprised burst of laughter. That struck him as so funny that he could not stop laughing! The more he tried to stop, the more he laughed, all the way down the hall! And I was right there laughing with him! It was the best tension reliever, and I went into surgery feeling ready.

When I woke up, I was told that the surgery had gone well and that I would be able to go home the next day. Other than an extreme sore throat caused by the surgical equipment that was placed in my throat during the procedure, I don't remember having too much pain to deal with. I did notice that I had no upper register in my voice whatsoever. When I tried humming to test my vocal cords, there was very little control there. My surgeon assured me that that was completely normal and that everything was fine. I just had to allow time for healing.

I'm happy to report that after approximately three months of vocal exercises and speaking affirmations such as "My throat is completely healed and I can sing better than I ever could before," I was able to return to joyously singing.

Extreme Gratitude!

I did receive some interesting news about my thyroid that made me look back on my journey and reflect on how everything had unfolded. I realized that everything that happened was a blessing and took place in perfect order.

After being removed, my thyroid was sent off for testing. It was discovered that there were cancer cells present, but they were in an area of the thyroid that was not the focus of the biopsies. If the original biopsies had produced results the way they were supposed to, the results would have shown that nothing was there, I would not have had my thyroid removed and the cancer cells would have gone unchecked. Thank God for incomplete testing!

If it hadn't been for the nosebleeds that got me to the doctor in the first place, I wouldn't have been sent to the ENT physician, who discovered the lump in my thyroid and ended up being the most amazing surgeon to handle my thyroid removal. I was divinely protected every step of the way without even realizing it! What a grand lesson in looking for the gift in every situation! Thank you, God!

More Pieces to the Puzzle

I achieved self-awareness on many levels from my thyroid experience. By actively looking at health issues in my body, I could see that they were a road map to what was going on in my thoughts and emotions. They were clues to the self-talk that I had allowed to become so ingrained in me I was unaware of it. I was grateful for this process.

Knowledge is power. By becoming aware of what we are doing, we then have the power to start making the necessary changes, keeping in mind that change is a process that requires time and conscious effort on our part to create the desired results. We can start the process by being gentle with ourselves, allowing the time it takes for self-reflection, creating new positive self-talk and taking things one day at a time, one moment at a time, doing the best we can and loving ourselves through it all.

Author Louise Hay offers an extensive list of possible metaphysical causes of different physical ailments in her book, *Heal Your Body*. She also offers a healing affirmation to go along with each symptom.

After looking up each one of my symptoms, I found the accuracy to be amazing. For thyroid problems, she offers the possible cause: "Humiliation. I never get to do what I want to do. When is it going to be my turn?" I so resonated with this. The accompanying affirmation she offers is: "I move beyond old limitations and now allow myself to express freely and creatively." Wow!

When I looked up my symptom of hypothyroidism, the book said, "Giving up. Feeling hopelessly stifled." The healing affirmation stated, "I create a new life with new rules that totally support me."

I was not able to locate the exact diagnosis of Hashimoto's thyroiditis on Louise Hay's list, but I found the generic *itis*, which states, "Anger and frustration about conditions you are looking at in your life." The accompanying affirmation states, "I am willing to change all patterns of criticism. I love and approve of myself."

I was so grateful to have discovered this information because it was a solid place to start understanding what was possibly going on within me. But I knew these were just suggestions and that any changes within myself that I wished to happen would come about through my conscious effort to understand myself and to work through any erroneous thoughts that I held as true.

After much contemplation, I came up with a few theories of my own. As I said earlier, Hashimoto's thyroiditis was explained to me as the immune system viewing the thyroid as a foreign object and attacking it. Maybe I was subconsciously angry at myself for years of silence, for not speaking up for myself. Thus, my immune system was attacking my center of communication.

We can be our own worst enemy by berating ourselves with negative self-talk. The body is listening. It hears every word we say, every thought we think and every emotion that we give power to. The body takes literally everything that we feed it, and it says, "Yes! I will get right on that!"

Thank you, God! What a wonderful gift this is, because the ability to create negative conditions in our bodies also means that we can create positive conditions in our bodies. Dare to imagine the effect of immersing yourself in unconditional self-love. You have the power to do this! It is a choice!

4

And Then There Were None

If you have ever been faced with the loss of a parent and all the feelings that brings up, you know how devastating that can be. But what happens when you lose your last remaining parent?

To Mom, with Love

Nine months after I had my thyroid removed, my mother, who was struggling with dementia, developed sepsis and died at the age of 79. For the last several years of her life, she had been living in a nursing home, unable to care for herself, at the mercy of this dark funk that was slowly claiming her memory.

It was hard to see my mother exist in this state of limbo. She had always been so present in her life. She raised four children who were her top priority; she instilled in each one of us a strong work ethic, manners, respect for our elders, kindness and basic human decency; and she wrapped it all up with a sense of humor. Even though she had a full-time job, she always made sure that her family had a home-cooked meal every night. She also made sure that each one of her children knew their way around the kitchen, be it cooking or cleaning. My sister and I were usually the ones who took turns doing the dishes, while my two brothers were responsible for all the outside work like mowing, trimming and taking out the trash. I remember when, one night after supper, Mom asked one of my brothers to do the dishes. He made the mistake of telling her that doing dishes was "a woman's work." Guess who did dishes that evening? My brother never made that statement again!

I have so many wonderful memories of the amazing woman who was my mom. She was room mother in my sixth-grade class, she stayed up all night sewing a dress for me when I had a singing solo at a high school competition and she got me my first real job when I was 18, at the same office where she worked—we ended up working together for many years. We were not only mother and daughter, we were friends. It has been an honor for me to share that type of relationship with her.

She spent her final years in one room at a nursing home with minimal participation in life. My brother and sister, who had lived with Dad, lovingly took turns seeing to her needs every week. My sister took it upon herself to do Mom's laundry and handle her finances. My youngest brother and I both lived farther away, but we each saw Mom as much as we could, and we were grateful beyond words for the loving care that our siblings extended to Mom on a regular basis.

Seven months before Mom passed away, the oldest of my two brothers bought a house with the understanding that my sister and I, along with my youngest daughter, who is autistic, would also move in, sharing expenses and looking out for each other. This arrangement has been a blessing to each one of us! We all get along, and our home is filled with much love and laughter.

We purchased a wheelchair for Mom so we could bring her to our house on holidays and for other family gatherings. Over the years, whenever she was with us, she tended to fall asleep, but the last couple of times that we brought her to our house, she was more alert. It was wonderful!

One of these occasions was her birthday, and her last visit was on Mother's Day. We came up with the idea of making the entire day about things that she absolutely loved to do. John Wayne was Mom's favorite actor, so on her birthday, we watched all her favorite John Wayne movies. She sat there all day with a smile on her face and never fell asleep at all. Although she did not talk much, the fact that she was showing an interest in something was huge! Our hearts were full as we enjoyed every minute spent with Mom that day.

When Mother's Day came around, we thought we would try it again, since the previous time had been so successful. Other of her movie favorites were ones that featured Rock Hudson and Doris Day. We made Mom her favorite meal of fried chicken, mashed potatoes, gravy and green beans. She ate every bit of her meal while watching her favorite movies on television. Again, she sat there the entire time with a smile on her face, and she never once dozed off. We didn't know it, but that would be the last time she would be in our home.

One month later, Mom got very sick and died. It happened quickly, in less than a week. The last couple of days, hospice stepped in and took care of her. They were so wonderful!

The night before Mom died, my sister and I spent the night with her in her room. Mom just laid there quietly. My sister and I are so goofy—I don't know how we got started, but something made us start laughing. From there, it progressed to us laughing uncontrollably at everything we said; we couldn't seem to stop. At one point, we heard a soft knocking on the door, and the hospice nurse poked her head in, asking if we were okay. She saw that we were laughing, which brought a relieved smile to her face. She went on to explain that the nurses had heard us, but they were not sure if we were laughing or crying. We apologized for being so loud and thanked the nurse for caring enough to check on us. Seeing that everything was okay, she checked on Mom, told us goodnight and quietly left the room. Of course, we were not finished laughing, but we did manage to eventually settle down to get some sleep.

Maybe it was our way of relieving all the stress we had been dealing with for the last few days. I like to think that Mom could hear every bit of our laughter and was maybe comforted by it. I was reminded of our experience of seeing Dad's smiling face the night before he passed away. That made me hopeful. It has been my experience that the lighter you can make those difficult moments of fear and sadness surrounding loved ones, the easier it is to move through the experience.

The next day, my brother, sister and I spent time with Mom while waiting for our youngest brother to arrive. When he was finally able to get to the hospital, we told him to go have some private time with Mom. He wasn't in there very long; when he came back out, he said he thought she was gone. We were so grateful that he was able to see her in time. We were also relieved, for Mom's sake, that she was no longer at the mercy of the dark fog that had stolen her memories. We were able to say goodbye to Mom and bless her on her journey.

Well, there I was, at the end of an era. Both of my parents had died. I can't tell you how many times I wish I could talk to them or see them, to give them one more hug and tell them I love them. This all hits home when they are no longer here.

And it's not just about parents. We all have people in our lives whom we love and would miss terribly if they were not here. If only we could just remember this while we are all wrapped up in our daily routines. Don't take anyone for granted. Make time for the people you love. You won't be sorry!

5

I Thought I Was Ready

Have you ever found yourself feeling ready to be in a relationship, but when faced with the opportunity, you found yourself falling back into old patterns, feeling like you've been there before?

Here I Go Again

I missed Mom terribly after she died, but I found myself feeling at peace with her passing. Maybe it was because I was getting older, or maybe it was because I had already lost so many family members to this process that is part of life. Regardless, I felt ready to shift my focus on moving forward with my life.

After a chance meeting about two months after Mom had passed away, I found myself in a brief relationship that was very reminiscent of my first marriage. It didn't start out that way, but by the time I figured out what I had gotten myself into, I was reliving all those old feelings of inadequacy that I thought I had worked through.

Why was I allowing myself to be part of this type of relationship again? I thought I had learned these lessons already. Maybe I was settling because I wanted to prove to myself that I was worthy of having a relationship. Or maybe a mismatched relationship was all that I felt I deserved. Looking back, I can see that all my lessons were crying out for me to look at how I felt about and valued myself.

Even when some lessons repeat themselves multiple times, I have observed that with each lesson comes more awareness. These are the baby steps. When you have spent your whole life feeling and thinking a certain way, total change is not going to happen overnight. Every step and every lesson is necessary, and there is no way around them. The only way is to go through them. Celebrate each lesson learned, and remember, *not* beating yourself up is *how* you can love yourself through every bit of it.

On one level, I did gain some insight. The more I thought about how I had felt emotionally throughout this relationship, the more I was reminded of the feelings I experienced in my first marriage. I thought I had worked through those feelings, but I realized that I had just stuffed them way down inside in my rush to get away from my first husband. Thank you, God, for guiding me to this most recent partner who helped bring all those emotions back to the surface to be healed. I was finally ready to really look at how I valued myself! What a gift!

Drawing from the Angels

I had an interesting experience right before I ended this last relationship. I love angels! I have several angel card decks, and when I have a question about something, need some guidance or just want some validation on a specific topic, I shuffle the cards while holding the question in my mind. I randomly draw at least three cards, and I find it amazing the answers I receive.

One night I was back in my bedroom with my angel cards, frantically shuffling them and asking them if leaving him was the right thing to do. But none of the cards seemed to be addressing the questions I had asked.

I have no recollection what two of the cards said. The third card spoke of going out in nature so my power animal could be revealed to me. I remember thinking to myself, "Well, that's not going to happen! I'm going to bed!"

The next morning, I went to work extremely early, like I always do. I'm usually the first one there, when it's still dark and only a few lights illuminate the parking lot. That morning, I wasn't thinking about anything in particular as I parked my car and got out. I was in the moment, enjoying the fresh air and quiet peacefulness of that early hour.

As I looked over at the grassy, landscaped area located a short distance from my car, I noticed two wild ducks walking along and minding their own business. I told them good morning and how beautiful I thought they were. I thanked them for showing up and wished them a wonderful day. I then walked to the door of the building, which was approximately 50 feet from my car. I happened to turn around before going inside and noticed that the ducks were no longer there. I stepped back into the parking lot and looked around. They had vanished! There had been no sound, no quacking, no flapping of wings. They were nowhere to be found!

I quickly went inside and immediately got on my phone to look up information about ducks, remembering what my angel card from the previous evening had said about power animals. I forget the exact way that I worded the question, but it was something like: What is the spiritual meaning of a duck? The first answer that popped up stated that just because I had a suitor, this did not mean he was who I was supposed to be with! As I read on, I was amazed at the significance of the symbology, which seemed to convey: Stop being a victim and take charge of the situation, stay out of situations in which you are defenseless and forced to do something that you're uncomfortable with, face something in your life that you've been avoiding so you can move on, seek balance in your emotional life, speak up for yourself and speak your truth. I'm sure my mouth dropped open in surprise!

Spirit knows me so well! It had to send me my power animal in an unguarded moment when my mind was neutral and contained no resistance. I would have never consciously thought of a duck as my power animal, but that was before I became informed.

I am grateful to Spirit for that mystical experience. I was shown that when we sincerely ask for answers and remain open to receive, they come to us via the path of least resistance and in any number of ways. We just need to trust and pay attention.

On a final note, the company I worked for had been in that building for years. I had never seen ducks there, and I never saw them again after that morning. You may draw your own conclusion about their presence on that specific day. I personally believe that they were intended for me, a message from the universe. Thank you, God!

6

I'm a What?

Have you ever asked the universe for answers about your life? What if you stayed so open to the possibility of receiving those answers that the answers came to you? Imagine, after just one discovery, so many things in your life suddenly making sense.

Finding Sacred "Me" Time

I worked a great distance from my home and had quite a long commute, which consisted of driving a total of four hours daily—two hours to work in the morning and two hours home in the evening. This was on top of working a ten-hour day. After also completing daily chores that had to be done and squeezing in a few hours of sleep, it did not take a math genius to figure out that I didn't have much time for anything else.

What about the things that my soul was crying out for? Time for reading, journaling, meditating, pampering myself and enjoying friends, family and playtime seemed beyond my reach, an impossible dream.

Sometimes in our lives, we set things up the way they need to be at the time, and this can't be helped. We do the best we can. We squeeze special moments in when possible. We keep going.

For a long time, my schedule was set in stone, non-negotiable. The only time out of my entire day when I was not actually "doing" something was the four hours of driving. I decided that since I was a captive audience for those four hours, I would fill that time with something meaningful and worthwhile.

I amassed a rather large collection of CDs of favorite books, self-help seminars by favorite authors and beautiful music. I also had a weekly practice CD of the music that my church band was working on. I spent many an hour rehearsing my music while I was driving.

It All Makes Sense Now

One of the things that kept me grounded during and after my most recent relationship was listening to the Hay House World Summit 2018. This set contains 100 CDs, which consist of hour-long interviews with various spiritual authors, life coaches, doctors and the like, on their own topic of expertise.

I made a pact with myself to listen to the CDs from beginning to end, in order, no matter how interesting one of the other ones may have sounded that was further on in the set. I soaked them all in, I was fed, and they became a bright spot, spilling over into my thoughts throughout the day.

I found the synchronicity of the topics that coincided with events in my daily life to be quite interesting. And I was about to learn exactly how amazing divine timing really was, how events in my life were occurring at precisely the right moment.

As I was going through my breakup, I listened to Christiane Northrup's lecture from her book titled *Dodging Energy Vampires*. Talk about divine timing! I was blown away! Christiane explained what energy vampires are and the behaviors they exhibit. She recited a lengthy list of things that they do within a relationship. She went on to explain that these types of people are attracted to the energy of a type of person called an empath. The empath characteristics that she listed described me to a tee.

This knowledge was a game changer for me. I wanted to learn more about this topic, so I went out and bought Christiane's book, which I highly recommend. It explained so much! Not only did it go into great detail about the characteristics of empaths, but it also went on to talk about what vampire/empath relationships are like, how to navigate through this type of relationship and how this type of unbalanced relationship can eventually cause health issues for the empath within that relationship. I found it interesting that thyroid disorders and autoimmune disorders were on the list, both of which I have.

Hit the Reset Button

Ever since I had listened to Christiane's lecture while on my commute to work and then after reading her book, I was amazed at my new self-knowledge. I am an empath! I found myself looking back over my life—my extreme sensitivity as a child, my tendency to cry all the time, my feelings of unworthiness and of having to earn any love received, my need to fix everything, constant giving but leaving myself out of the equation, feeling and taking on other people's energy, and perfectionism.

Having a new understanding of what had been going on throughout my life, I found myself having compassion for this little soul who had been doing the best that she knew how. I was finally able to embrace her with love.

The good news is that, along with gaining the knowledge of what I am, there is also much information available for empaths about tools for navigating through life in the highest and best possible way, protecting one's energy, being the lightworkers that we inherently are and learning how to use the gifts that we have been given.

For all who are now reading my words, if you are not currently living your dream, I encourage you to search your own heart and find what it is that you truly love to do. This is an internal journey, different for each person. Discover what your gifts are and find the courage to travel the path that calls to your soul, the path that makes your heart sing. We are each unique, with our own gifts to offer. Be true to yourself. Be authentic. I love you!

7

Back to Basics

Know this! It is never too late to reinvent oneself!

What Do I Want?

This seems like such a simple question. But after I discovered that I was an empath, I found myself in uncharted territory. Did I even know what I wanted? Did I believe that it's even possible to have it? And last, did I believe that I deserved it?

This journey called life is like peeling back the layers of an onion. There is always something to think about, to discover, to learn. We are never finished.

There is great freedom in this. We have the freedom to change our minds, to try again, and we can choose to see it all as a grand adventure...or not. Using this precious gift of free will that we have been given, life truly is what we make it. We may not have control over everything that shows up, but we have total control over how we choose to respond to everything.

I had already been through so many difficult, challenging events in my life, and with confidence in my ability to further navigate, I continued to push through all the additional lessons presented to me. I was grateful for the strength and courage that I gained from having gone through every bit of it. Moving forward, I decided that I would give myself permission to be open to new experiences and to learning new things.

Divine Ideas: What if...?

I still enjoyed pulling angel cards to see what the heavenly realms had to say about my life. I do want to say that, for a while, there had been a distinct pattern in the messages being revealed to me. Two things were coming through with great regularity: writing as a part of my life's purpose and also being continuously told that I am a lightworker, an earth angel. My angel cards also suggested multiple times that I study energy work, such as Reiki, to develop skills to be a practitioner.

As an empath, I found these possibilities so intriguing. It was also confirmation of an idea that had been calling to me for the last couple of years, a voice that kept saying, "Write a book."

I don't remember when this idea first showed up. It felt like it had somehow always been a part of me, sometimes persistently in the forefront and sometimes silently waiting on the back burner, but always waiting for me to breathe life into it.

There were times when I would try to figure out what I could possibly write about. Different topics would flit through my mind, yet nothing felt right. The idea would then recede. After a while, something occurred to me. In all those moments of contemplation, I had never said "Yes."

"Okay, universe! I will write a book!" Once I committed to this, ideas started pouring out of me. I guess I just needed to give myself permission. It was as if the floodgates had been opened. I kept writing everything down, intending to sort it all out later.

Over time, a subject theme emerged in my writing— the difficult times I had been through in my life and all the positive things that saw me through it all. I wrote them all down, and I knew what I needed to do. I felt in my heart that I was to write of my journey in life, how I got through the difficult times and the lessons I had learned.

I will never forget a powerful message I received from Spirit that communicated that I was on the right track. I was the records administrator for my company's human resources department. We were a government contractor, and I was the point of contact for agents who would come in periodically to review personnel files. My job was to escort them to a private room when they arrived and escort them back to the front door when they were finished.

One day, as I escorted an agent back to the front door, he mentioned that he was a published author. I told him I wanted to write a book. How odd is that?

The next few times the agent came in to review files, we would talk briefly about writing. I enjoyed those conversations when he came to visit. Then one day, I was told that someone was up front to see me. When I went to see who it was, it was the agent. He asked me, as we were standing at the entrance, what I intended to write my book about. When I told him that it was going to be about my journey and the positive things that had happened that got me through hard times, his exact words to me were, "The Holy Spirit told me to come here today and tell you that that is what you're supposed to write your book about." Well, you could have knocked me over with a feather!

In the weeks and months that followed, if I found myself procrastinating in my writing, I would remember the divine message that I had received and pick up my pen again. When Spirit speaks, it's probably a good idea to listen.

New Paths to Follow

One thing that was totally new to me was the study of Reiki. I knew that a friend of mine at church was a Reiki Master, so, from conversations that we had, I was aware that Reiki is energy work. But I didn't really know details about it. After I had received the messages from my angel cards, I felt that Reiki was something that I was being guided to learn more about. When I mentioned my interest to my friend, she informed me that she had a Reiki I class coming up soon. Without hesitation, I signed up.

Since giving myself permission to try new things, I was finding new courage forming within me, courage to say yes. I was feeling a sense of excitement about life in general.

The day came for my Reiki I class. I learned the background of Reiki, what a natural process it is, and that we all inherently have the capability to perform it.

I learned how to open up to this process and had the opportunity to practice on fellow students during class. I even got to the point where I could feel energy in the palms of my hands. I loved every minute of it! By the end of the day, I had my certificate. In the big picture, I had no idea where this would lead, but there was no doubt in my mind that this was something I was meant to do.

On the second Sunday of every month after the service, my church conducted a Reiki circle for anyone who wanted to participate in receiving energy work. The day after my Reiki class happened to be Reiki circle Sunday and, because I had successfully completed Reiki I, I was invited to join the other Reiki practitioners in performing Reiki on the people sitting within the circle.

I remember right before the session was about to get started, I was feeling unsure and was questioning myself whether I was ready to do this yet. I was about to bow out when one of the other practitioners turned on the most beautiful etherical music. The palms of my hands immediately started vibrating, and I knew I had to participate.

I have not missed a Sunday Reiki circle since. I have received much positive feedback from people whom I have performed Reiki on, and I have gone on to complete and receive my certificate for Reiki II. I continue to practice on friends and family, preparing for the day when I can complete Reiki III and become a Reiki Master.

As I continue opening myself to the energy within me, thus increasing my healing Reiki ability, I feel so grateful for all I have learned. I have discovered that I have gifts within me that I can share with the world.

By going within and working on aspects of myself that needed healing, I not only learned the life lessons that my soul needed, but I was now teaching by example. When we each shine our own unique light, that gives others permission to shine theirs as well. From all my spiritual studies, I believe we are all on this planet to be of service to others, and Reiki is just one of many ways that I, personally, can contribute to the good of the whole.

Just the Beginning

Through the course of this book, I have taken you down the many paths I have traveled and have exposed some of my most vulnerable moments. I look back and realize, with gratitude, that everything I have experienced has provided a gift. It has all served a purpose and contributed to who I am today. Nothing has been wasted.

I challenge you, dear reader, to look within your own heart, to find those places that need healing and love. Courageously, dare to rewrite your own story, and then pay it forward by sharing with others how you did that so they can learn from your example. Be the light!

Moving forward, if I can write a book at the age of 64 and see it through to publication while holding down a full-time job, if I can study the energy work called Reiki and become a Master at that, what else can I accomplish? The answer is: absolutely anything I put my mind to! I have even started taking guitar lessons. If it calls to my heart and soul, if it feels right, I am open. No more fear! I feel like I am finally living life on my terms! Thank you, God!

Suggested Authors

Louise Hay

Wayne Dyer

Esther and Jerry Hicks

Don Miguel Ruiz

Deepak Chopra

Eckhart Tolle

Alan Cohen

Christiane Northrup

Matt Kahn

Gabrielle Bernstein

Printed in the United States
By Bookmasters